From Serdije Ade...
to Cheryl 5-2...

# The Soul in Love

# The Soul in Love

CLASSIC POEMS OF

ECSTASY AND EXALTATION

*Edited with New English Versions by*
DEEPAK CHOPRA

HARMONY BOOKS
*New York*

Published by Harmony Books, New York, New York.

Random House, Inc. New York, Toronto, London, Sydney, Auckland
www.randomhouse.com

HARMONY BOOKS is a registered trademark and the Harmony Books
colophon is a trademark of Random House, Inc.

Printed in the United States of America

Design by Jennifer Ann Daddio

Library of Congress Cataloging-in-Publication Data

The soul in love : classic poems of ecstasy and exaltation / edited with new
English versions by Deepak Chopra.
1. Sufi poetry, Persian—Translations into English. I. Chopra, Deepak.
PK6480.E5 S68 2001
891—dc21
00-044908

ISBN 0-609-60648-4

10 9 8 7 6 5 4 3 2 1

First Edition

# Contents

*Introduction*  9

*About These New Versions*  25

Rumi  27

Hafiz  47

Kabir  57

Mirabai  75

Rabindranath Tagore  85

# Introduction

ॐ

There is a rare experience that can bring more delight than falling in love— falling in love with God. Both are mysteries of the soul. We are used to living our lives without touching such mysteries. Falling in love may remain in the back of our minds as a supremely desirable event, but the world doesn't revolve around it, except for lovers. We give them a privileged position, briefly exempt from care and worry. Life's business gets suspended while lovers sigh and long for each other, feeding off the mere touch of the beloved, intoxicated by a glance or a word. Glances and words aren't really magical, yet love makes them feel that way.

The excitement of falling in love always comes to an end, and when it does, the mystery fades. Day by day, the intoxication is less, and soon the lovers get welcomed back into the reality of business as usual. Yet a privileged few are spared this return to everyday life and remain in love seemingly without end. For this to happen, the beloved must be God. All other loves pale beside a sacred one. Saints and sages alike tell us one story over and over of being irresistibly drawn to God's embrace:

> Oh God
> I have discovered love!
> How marvelous, how good, how beautiful it is! . . .
> I offer my salutation
> To the spirit of passion that aroused
>     and excited this whole universe
> And all it contains.

These words are from Rumi, the sublime Persian poet so enraptured with God that he clung to a pole outside his house, swinging back and forth in ecstasy. From his lips poured joyous, drunken words about his Beloved, but these words weren't the ordinary effusions of a lover seeing through rose-colored glasses—Rumi was a lover who had seen something at the depths of life. To him, God was everywhere, and every atom of the universe pulsated with the same divine rapture. The power that created the cosmos poured through Rumi's veins, and the experience was not all pleasure. It was earthshaking:

> You go to bed crying and wake up the same,
> You plead for what doesn't come
> Until it darkens your days.
> You give away everything, even your mind,
> You sit down in the fire, wanting to become ashes,
> And when you meet with a sword,
> You throw yourself on it.

Ordinary people (the villagers and devotees who surrounded Rumi) were reluctant to throw themselves into such a frenzied state, but they were fascinated by Rumi. In mesmerized groups they stood around while he swung on his pole rhapsodizing, or whirled in the dance of the dervishes and sang, because his songs and verses were inspired. It is that quality which puts God-intoxication above falling in love. Some aspect of wisdom is present, not a mere emotion or inflamed passion. Reading Rumi, a chill runs up your spine because you have the uncanny feeling that you have been where he is. Perhaps he is even yourself:

> Motes of dust dancing in the light
> That's our dance, too.
> We don't listen inside to hear the music—
> No matter.
> The dance goes on, and in the joy of the sun
> Is hiding a God

Rumi was dancing the dance of life. He knew it, and so did his listeners, which is why the line between poet, saint, and lover became quite blurry in his case. No poet is more intimate than Rumi, no lover more crazed, no saint more innocent. An air of the supernatural gathered around him because he never lost this wild, extreme state of ecstasy. Somehow the deepest lovers don't have to fear time. Their intoxication is permanent, even though the divine beloved is invisible, remote, and never touched physically.

Centuries ago an Indian princess named Mirabai walked away from wealth and privilege to live among the poor just so she could remain intoxicated. Like Rumi, Mirabai expresses amazement that the rest of us don't follow her lead. But to do that requires great strength, for the life of God-intoxication leaves no room for compromise, as Mira points out time and again:

I am going mad with pain—but no one gets it.
Only the wounded feel their wounds,
    embracing the fire in their hearts.
Only the jeweler knows the worth of the jewel,
    not the one who tosses it aside.
Mira wanders the forest, sick with love.
Her pain will only cease when the Dark One comes
    to heal it.

These lines are as intimidating as they are alluring. What is such a love, and why do certain people fall so deeply under its spell?

I have been fascinated by such questions for a long time, and I found answers only by going into the soul-places where mortal love and immortal love meet. Romeo and Juliet were mortal and even died for love, yet they attained a kind of immortality by being allowed to live on in verse. Immortal love doesn't need poetry. However, it is our good fortune that some of the God-intoxicated have written words that permit access into their ecstatic world. Particularly in the East, in that exotically woven belt of lands that stretches from Arabia to the Indian subcontinent, poets and saints are never far apart. Mirabai and Rumi are only two such figures; there are many, many more. In this collection I have gathered a few of the most revered, beginning in the medieval period and extending to this century. The name of Rumi has gathered much luster recently, but the others—Kabir, Hafiz, Tagore, and Mirabai—deserve just as much recognition. In their own cultures they stand as beacons of inspiration, largely because the common people have taken them into their hearts and continue to sing their words every day.

From my childhood I remember women gathering in my grandmother's house in Delhi, often accompanied by a wheezing little harmonium, and the voices of family and friends raised to praise God in the words of Kabir or Mirabai. In that setting there was no question about whether this was "great" poetry; it was great in its heartfelt yearning, for much of this writing is the purest yearning imaginable:

> Take me to that place where no one can go
> Where death is afraid
> And swans alight to play
> On the overflowing lake of love.
> There the faithful gather
> Ever true to their Lord.

This is Mirabai, but the amorous theme she touches on is widely shared. Mystics either remain speechless, or they drift toward the language of lovers. There seems to be no middle ground. If they speak as lovers, we still hear all the complaints of earthly love, that it is fickle, that it brings sleepless nights and empty days, that food has no savor when the lover is gone and the heart becomes anxious and restless. In a way it seems strange to keep using such language about God, because the key quality of immortal love is freedom. It isn't bound by time and space; it doesn't really need expression or outward show because nothing is happening outwardly. The soul's love occurs when a person goes to an unchanging place beyond all dimensions. As Kabir says:

> A man lives inside boundaries
> His spirit lives outside.
> Something else knows neither one.

Like Mirabai and Rumi, Kabir lived in the so-called medieval period (his dates are roughly 1440–1518), a term that is too Western to really make sense in India, where unbroken traditions span many centuries. He was low-born, trained in the family craft of weaving. Because cultural boundaries are inescapable, mystical poets still acquire religious labels. Rumi is therefore considered Muslim and Mirabai Hindu, but Kabir refused to be labeled, and was claimed by both religions. (If you read deep enough, these poets easily embrace all faiths. For example, there are mentions of Christ throughout Rumi.) The charming tale of what happened to Kabir's body after he died is known by every Indian child: After he passed on, Kabir's remains were claimed by both the Hindus and Muslims of the town. One side wanted to cremate him and scatter his ashes over a holy place, while the other wanted a burial. The disagreement between the two factions grew heated to the brink of violence. There seemed to be no peaceful solution until Kabir came in a dream and told his followers to open his casket. When they did, Kabir's body was gone, miraculously changed into a bundle of flowers. One faction took half the flowers and burned them; the other took their half and buried them. Thus both faiths got what they wanted, and Kabir became storied as a saint who could not be trapped by orthodoxy on either side.

Delightful as it is to spend time with these divine lovers, I have also come to believe that the God-mad (to use a wonderful phrase from India) have hit upon a truth that has objective validity: There really is a place beyond time and space that we can access even though we are here inside time and space. Modern physics speaks of the "event horizon," which lies beyond the travel of light, a place that must exist but can never be seen because the oldest photons in the universe are unable to bring us any data about it. When you ask a question like, "What happened before time began?" or "Where did things exist before the universe was created?" you are not making sense on this side of the event horizon. There is no time before time began and no place outside space. Yet to a quantum physicist, all such questions do make sense if you cast your mind over the event horizon. Thus we hear about additional dimensions that once existed, about mega-universes that might have served as incubators for our own, and so on. The space beyond space is called "virtual" in the terms of physics; it is an empty place, completely black and cold (words that aren't really meaningful outside our universe), yet filled with the potential to create all time, space, matter, and energy.

The womb of creation is over the event horizon, and it is very real. The Big Bang erupted from virtual space. In other words, so did space-time itself. The amazing implication is that creation didn't happen at a particular moment. You can run a clock backward to try to get to the exact second that the Big Bang occurred, but just when you are about to arrive at the birth of things, your clock will falter and cease. All events will become compacted into a density too heavy and concentrated to allow for either time or space. Properties like weight and size, duration and movement disappear. At this point of seeming nothingness, everything is possible. Every single second of the life of the cosmos—past, present, and future—coheres into a unity. This point has been called a singularity by physics, but mystics call it God. God is the One and Only, the All that is only itself yet contains diverse creation. The mystic's God is not a person or a place but a state that is everywhere at once. This abstract portrayal remains true even when God is being named as father or mother, lover or friend—these are just words used in an attempt to humanize the ineffable.

To cross the event horizon seems physically impossible, yet it is spiritually our birthright. The poets in this book exercised that right, approaching God with awe and trembling but with disarming intimacy, as if meeting the One was the most natural thing in the world. Who is to say that they are wrong? Perhaps messages are drifting across the event horizon all the time. Rabindranath Tagore, the great Bengali poet and Nobel laureate, took the ecstatic tradition of Kabir and Mirabai into our time, going so far as to translate Kabir as an act of homage. Tagore had a famous meeting with Einstein in which the two compared their sense of what God's reality might be, but it is in his poetry that Tagore speaks most wistfully of how easy it is to miss the divine fragrance that is all around us. He uses the image of a flower that has been passed by on the road:

When the lotus opened, I didn't notice and went
away empty-handed.

Only now and again do I suddenly sit up from my
  dreams to smell a strange fragrance. It comes on
  the south wind, a vague hint that makes me ache
  with longing, like the eager breath of summer
  wanting to be completed. I didn't know what
  was so near, or that it was mine.

This perfect sweetness blossoming in the depths of
  my heart.

Tagore is the tenderest and most emotionally delicate of
the poets in this book—at least that is how he strikes me.
They all speak to our souls with the same uncanniness that I
mentioned earlier, but after a while one detects a definite
flavor from each: Rumi is sharp and challenging, the ever-
alert mind who gets impatient with the sleepy. Hafiz,
another great lyricist in Islamic poetry, often adopts the
metaphor of being drunk on wine, carelessly letting loose
his rapture in the "sin" of drinking and carousing. Mirabai
is the besotted slave of love, longing in the night for her
Dark Lord. (She uses oblique names for him, such as "lifter
of mountains," drawing from the legends about Krishna,

who is called dark because he is envisioned by his devotees as having deep blue or even black skin.) Kabir is harder to typify in my mind, perhaps because I grew up hearing him the way a churchgoer in this country hears hymns. He can be intimate, devoted, humble or haughty, detached, and even abrasive.

The God-mad are inevitably elusive; they don't know their place in society because they don't have one anymore. Therefore they feel free to speak in any way they choose. Mirabai is ironically aware of how much distress she is causing to conventional people by her divine love affair:

> The whole town thought I had gone mad.
> She'll ruin the family, my mother-in-law cried,
> And the prince sent me a cup of poison.
> I laughed as I drank it—don't they understand?
> Can you lose your body and mind
> If the Dark One has already taken them?

Naturally, the answer to her question is both yes and no. So-called sane people don't go dancing through the street, swinging on poles, or stripping naked before God, yet we still understand at a deeper level why such behavior defies sanity. We are all tuned in beyond the event horizon. Rumi puts it very simply in two lines that strike to the core of the ever-fleeting mystery:

> When you feel most alive, find out why.
> This is one guest you won't greet twice.

In one couplet he states the spiritual purpose of life, which is to find the essence, the seed of joy that permeates our most awake moments without ever being able to be caught and put in a bottle. This joy is the guest we can't greet twice, because it lives in the moment and is new every time. The miracle is that we greet it at all, yet we do. As simple as Rumi's words sound, he can turn on an instant and plumb the profound depths of mystical experience:

> He is the tree, the fruit, and the shade
> He is the sun, the light, and the dream
> The word and its meaning
> A point in the All
> Form in the formless
> Infinity in a void.

These words come at us with startling authority, and indeed all these poets seem to throw cosmic truth in our face with the same attitude: "I dare you to say I'm wrong."

More than ever, present-day society sorely misses the ecstasy and innocence that makes truth-telling so invaluable. Crossing the event horizon isn't merely a sojourn of joy and rapture—this unborn, unceasing, invisible virtual womb is where we come from. It is source and origin. If you have no experience of the one truly sacred place, you cannot claim to be fully human, not in the highest sense. To be fully human has always meant going beyond being human. Only then can a flesh-and-blood lover claim to transcend death.

Reading the poems in this book gives me renewed hope that the soul-journey is always open. The soul is that part of ourselves that doesn't believe in death and therefore never dies. I offer each verse in that spirit, and I have unshakable confidence that a huge mass of people feels the same yearning to go beyond, quickened by every line written here. It will be our fate to walk the pathless path one day, and as we do—or even before—it helps to know that the ones who will be waiting to guide us on that road are so wise and full of joy.

# About These New Versions

❦

For many readers, meeting these exotic poets from Persia and India will be a new experience, and I wanted to make it a thrilling one. The beauty of reading a Rumi or a Mirabai is that even across the span of centuries, we can feel their intense devotion enter into their love-filled world. Each poet has a unique voice in Persian, Bengali, or Hindi, but my aim here is not to re-create that voice literally. (The one exception is Tagore, who was such a brilliant translator of himself into English that I have deliberately—and humbly—tried to retain his own voice.) The spirit of poetry is rarely found in literal translations. Instead I have chosen to seek out the lyrical and joyous heart of the verse, first by reading from various scholarly sources, then re-creating each poem in a new and original version.

If you feel moved, if you inhale the air that spirit breathes, then your response will be the same as mine when I first stepped into the wondrous world of these great souls who found expression through poetry. In short, I want your soul to fall in love, just as mine and theirs did.

# Rumi

## (1207–1273)

☙❧

Perhaps the most revered of Sufi poets, Rumi was the inspiration for the sect known in the west as the "whirling dervishes," who imitate his ecstatic dancing. Rumi's poems were often created spontaneously as he danced and were copied down by disciples. He composed tens of thousands of poems in praise of his own spiritual master, using him as a symbol for the divine beloved. Among his works are countless aphorisms as well as epic poetry.

# Infatuation

ভৈ

Existence was born
When we fell in love with emptiness.

# On Fire

&c.

A candle was made to turn into flame
In one moment of destruction
That leaves no shadow.

# A Single Note

&c.

With a single note the nightingale
Makes me notice the rose
Falling into that place
Where everything is music.

# How Will I Know?

❦

You miracle-seekers are always wanting signs
So where are they?

Go to bed crying and wake up the same,
Plead for what doesn't come
Until it darkens your days.
Give away everything, even your mind,
Sit down in the fire, wanting to become ashes,
And when you meet with a sword,
Throw yourself on it.

Fall into the habit of such helpless mad things—
You will have your sign.

# In Silence

In love that is new—there must you die,
Where the path begins on the other side.
Melt into the sky and break free
From the prison whose walls you must smash.
Greet the hue of day
Out of a fog of darkness.
Now's the time!
Sneak out and die—
Silence will be the sign
That you've done it.
Everything else is just escaping from silence.
Now the moon can appear
In its quiet fullness.

# The Dance

Motes of dust dancing in the light
That's our dance, too.
We don't listen inside to hear the music—
No matter.
The dance goes on, and in the joy of the sun
Is hiding a God
Who teaches us to whirl.

# A Ruby

In the earliest dawn two lovers awoke
And sipping some water she said,
"Who do you love more,
Me or yourself?"
She wanted the truth.

So he replied, "I can't love myself,
I don't exist anymore.
I'm like a ruby held up to the sun
Melting into one redness.
Can you tell the gem from the world
When a ruby gives itself to sunlight?"

That's how holy ones can truthfully say
I am God.
So be a ruby at dawn
And hold to your practice.
Keep up the work, digging your well
Until you strike water.
Hang a ruby in your ear

And it will be the sun.
Keep knocking at the door
And joy will look out the window
To let you in.

## The Open Door

<br>

People are constantly crossing over
The threshold of eternity.
The door is open
If you can stay awake.

# Come with Me

၆၁

Come, let us go to the orchard in spring
Where sunlight and flowers mix with the wine.
None of this will matter if you don't meet me there,
None of this will matter if you do.

# Blossoming

Sunlight spreads over a face in the shadows
Like the flower of truth beginning to unfold.

# Rain

I feel like the earth
Astonished at fragrance
Borne in the air,
Made pregnant with mystery
From a drop of rain.

# Inscription

☙❧

This day knows itself
Beyond what words can tell,
Like passing a cup on which is written
*Life is mine, but not mine.*

# Reproof

Why boast of your strength?
The same wind that can topple a tree
Caresses the grass.

# Allowing for Love

Let lovers be crazy, disgraceful, and wild
Those who fret about such things
Aren't in love.

## Night Sounds

Through the night comes a frail, wavering song.
The moment I can't hear it
I will be gone.

# Intimacy

&c.

We spend the night in painful talk
As you dig out the secrets I wouldn't give.
So much depends on whether we love—
Let this night be over
And begin again.

# Unloved

Have you seen the kind
Who settle for less?
Who creep into corners
Just big enough for one?
They are unopened letters
Whose message is this:
Live! Live! Live!

# Hafiz

## (1325–1389)

❦

A Persian poet in the Sufi tradition, Hafiz taught
the Koran and held court posts. His subject mat-
ter was often worldly, reflecting the life around
him of hunting, drinking, and other pleasures.
Beneath the surface his subject is union with
God, in keeping with his mystical roots. His writ-
ings contain teachings, aphorisms, and songs as
well as poetry.

## What Has Been Given

&#x26A8;

When you were born God brought you so many gifts
 That you will never open them all.
Love's voice keeps saying, "Everything I have is yours."
So why do you still feel this pain?
Your soul long ago drowned in the middle of a vast sea
 While you pretend to be thirsty.
Life's infinite song pours through you
 Yet you hold your breath to squeeze it inside.
God kisses you awake every morning
 But you insist on sleeping and sleeping.
Hafiz can only smile.

# Losing Yourself

ॐ

To really lose yourself is like holding a gun to your head
　　And pulling the trigger—it takes courage.
Facing the truth means tying a bag over your head
　　Until you suffocate—it takes faith.
You have to be brave to follow God's tracks into the unknown
　　Where so many new things overwhelm and panic you.
But trust me and plunge the jeweled dagger into your heart.
This is what it takes to lose yourself.
There is no other path back to God.

## Impermanence

&&

When a lover of God gets ready to dance
The earth draws back and the sky trembles
Because his feet could stomp with such wild joy
That the sun, moon, and stars might tumble down
Dearest, the world should be seen as just this fragile
A speck, a nothing against the greater reality
And everything we perceive should be accepted
Like a toy carelessly dropped from a baby's hand
As it sleeps on, peacefully nestled in God.

# True Love

❦

When the mind becomes like a beautiful woman
It bestows all that you want of a lover.
Can you go that deep?
Instead of making love in the body
With other children of God,
Why not seek the true Lover
Who is always in front of you
With open arms?
Then you will be free of this world at last
Like me.

# Blessing

⊗⊗

We are all great rivers flowing to their end
Swirling inside us is the silt of ages and creatures and lands
And rain that has fallen for millions of years.
All this makes us cloudy with mud
Unable to see God.
As we struggle for clarity and the open sky
The Lord keeps saying the same thing:
Come to me now and be blessed,
Come.

# Purpose

ॐ

Time is a factory where everyone slaves away
Earning enough love to break their own chains.

# Awe

If you tried to paint a picture of my heart, or of God
It could never be beautiful enough.

# Etiquette

How should two people treat each other
  If they both know God?
Like a musician touching his violin
  With utmost care
  To caress the final note.

# Kabir

(1440–1518)

❦

He was a weaver born near Banar in north India.
Though Muslim by birth, he fused the mysticism
of the Sufis and the fervor of the *bhaktas* (wor-
shipers who use personal devotion as a path to
God). Kabir wrote in Hindi for the common
people and is still revered by them, especially
through his songs.

# The Sacred Fire

What is this flame raging with no fuel?
I saw it born when you set fire to the world.
I saw it spread, even in water,
Though no one can tell how.
While the city goes up in smoke,
The watchman sleeps contentedly, mumbling,
"My house is safe—let the rest turn to ashes."
Lord, how your colors flash!
Can I find satisfaction anywhere but in the fire?
Yet even as I think of this, I am born over and over,
Perpetually driven on.
No one is more lost than he who sees this fire
But pretends he doesn't.

Kabir says: "Is there any way out for such a one?"

# Spontaneity

When you feel most alive, find out why.
This is one guest you won't greet twice.

## Seeking

&&

Why run around sprinkling holy water?
There's an ocean inside you, and when you're ready
You'll drink.

# Unboundedness

൵

A man lives inside boundaries
His spirit lives outside.
Something else knows neither one.

# Merging

❦

A drop melting into the ocean—
That you can see.
The ocean melting into a drop—
Who sees that?

# The Answer

※

If you're so wise, ask God himself:
Who is the master and what does he teach?

Seek the child
Of a barren woman,
A fatherless son,
A soldier with no mount
Who fights without sword,
A scent with no flower,
A tree with no trunk,
A temple without deity,
Worship without offering,
A wingless wasp,
An empty cup
That overflows.

Only the valorous gain this peak—
The rest are scorched to nothing in the flame.
(A flame with no lamp!)
Understand? If you do, hooray!—
Kabir has departed into God.

# Seeing This . . .

He is the tree, the fruit, and the shade
He is the sun, the light, and the dream
The word and its meaning
A point in the All
Form in the formless
Infinity in a void.

Kabir saw all this
And was blessed.

# Take Me!

ॐ

The swan is the bearer
of an ancient tale—
Where does he come from?
Where does he fly?
What does he seek?
Where does he rest?

O swan, arise and follow me!
To that land free of sorrow
Knowing not death
Where the woods are in bloom
And the scented air says,
"I am He!"
The bee of the heart is drowning there
In nectar beyond all other joy

## Looking Within

ଚ୧

Where the moonlight of the Hidden One shines,
There beats the rhythm of life and death
There rapture wells forth, radiant with light
There unstruck music is heard, filling the three worlds
There a million lamps are burning as sun and moon
There the lover sways in joy to the beat of his drum
    light showers down
    and the worshiper is drunk with heavenly nectar.
See, death is not separate from life,
The right and left hand are the same.


Kabir says: "The learned have nothing to tell us,
Such wisdom is never written down."

# The Sorrowless Land

Following a path that couldn't be followed
I came to the sorrowless land.
The mercy of the Lord was upon me.
Though he is called unattainable,
I saw Him without sight.

Kabir says: "Reaching this land,
The ignorant grow wise,
The wise fall speechless with silence,
The worshiper becomes utterly drunk.
Made perfect in wisdom and detachment,
One breathes in with love, and with love breathes out."

# Bliss

## I

Where the sky is filled with music,
Made without fingers or strings.
Where the game of pleasure and pain
Never ends.
Kabir says: "When your life is merged
With the ocean of Life,
You will find your existence
In the land of bliss."

## II

There is a frenzy of ecstasy
In every hour,
As you squeeze out and drink
Each drop of the All.
Kabir says: "This is how to get beyond fear
And the mistake of life and death
Is left far behind."

## III

Awake, my heart
Your master is near.
Run to the beloved
So close by your drowsy head.
Having slept for ages without number,
Isn't this the morning to wake up?

# Upward

What a secret splendor
Is the mansion of the sky.
No one talks about the sun
Rising or setting.
In the ocean of manifestation,
Which is only love,
Day and night are felt as one,
Joy is forever, without a trace of sorrow.
There have I witnessed
The play of bliss.

## Nowhere to Go

ॐ

I asked my heart,
Where are you bound?
There's no traveler ahead of you
Or even a road.
How can you get there,
And where will you stay?
With no water, no boat,
No boatman, no shore.
No earth and no sky,
No time, no thing.

Lacking a body or a mind
Can the soul fill its thirst?
Don't stand on that ground of
Emptiness.
Be strong, O my heart,
Put your fancy away,
And stand where you are
In yourself.

# Open the Window

ର

When evening shadows fall thick and deep,
Love in darkness envelops us.
Open your window, be lost in the sky,
Drink deep of the heart's nectar,
Let the waves wash over you—
How splendid to feel the sea!
The sound of bells is rising.
Now behold, my brother,
The Lord is in thy body!

# Him

My Lord shows himself
and then he hides.
He binds me in chains
but gives me unlimited life.
He inspires words of sorrow
then words of joy.
He it is who heals all this strife,
And even though I give up my life,
Never will I forget Him.

## No One Can Tell Me

ↁↂ

A bird is dancing with the joy of life.

Where did it come from? No one can tell me.

What is it singing? No one can say.

It nests in the dark

Where the deep shade is thrown,

Coming at evening, departing at dawn,

Giving no clue to whatever it means.

I can't find out why this bird

Sits inside me,

On the branch of the Eternal—

Unnoticed by all—

In the shadow of love.

# Mirabai or Mira Bai

(1500–1550)

ॐ

Born and raised as a princess in Rajasthan, Mira was betrothed to a Rajput ruler. Tradition holds that after his death, since she considered Krishna to be her true husband, Mira began a life of holy wandering. She danced and sang her songs among the common people as an impoverished *bhakta*. The Dark Lord of her poems is Krishna, and in her vision God is an intensely personal lover.

# All Is Still

All at once the sight of you!
Your gaze, full of light,
Makes everything still—
Everything still.

The milk spills on the ground
My parents and brothers cry Stop!
"Pluck him from your heart," they say.
"Or your way is lost."

Mira says, "Who of you but him
Can really see into the dark well of my heart?"

# Refuge

That dark dweller in holy places
   is my only refuge.

O my companion,
What an illusion is worldly comfort—
   the moment you hold it, it goes.
I have chosen the Indestructible One instead.
The snake of death will not devour him.
My beloved dwells in my heart,
I have seen into that abode of joy
   where Mira takes shelter, my Lord,
   to be your slave.

# Passion's Fruit

How sweet were the plums
The desert girl bit into
Until she found one fit to offer Him.
She chewed and sucked on it first,
This awkward, dirty, low-born girl.
Yet God took the fruit she held out to him—
Because she was offering her love.
She couldn't tell splendor from dust
   but she'd tasted the nectar of passion.
She didn't know a word of scripture,
   but a chariot swept her away
To swing in heavenly ecstasy, tied to her God.

Mira says: "The Lord of the fallen
Will save anyone who can find such rapture."

# Come Back!

The love that binds me to you, O Lord,
   is unbreakable
Like a diamond that smashes the hammer
   when it is struck.

Like polish seeping into gold
   my heart has seeped into you,
Like the lotus rising from the water
   my life rises from you,
Like the night bird gazing at the passing moon
   I am lost dwelling on you.

O my beloved—come back!

# This Pain of Love

&

### I.

I am going mad with pain—but no one gets it.
Only the wounded feel their wounds,
    embracing the fire in their hearts.
Only the jeweler knows the worth of the jewel,
    not the one who tosses it aside.
Mira wanders the forest, sick with love.
Her pain will only cease when the Dark One comes to heal it.

### II.

His flute sounds over the river—
Music snatches away my mind,
My senses are cut loose to wander
    toward dark waters.
I bend to hear his music
And my body vanishes.
O Lord who can lift mountains,
Come quick and take away this ache!

## Where Love Is First

Take me to that place where no one can go
Where death is afraid
And swans alight to play
On the overflowing lake of love.
There the faithful gather
Ever true to their Lord
Refining their love in the fire of the mind—
Arrayed in goodness, adorned with ankle bells,
They dance the dance of contentment,
They crown themselves with a crown of gold
There where love of the Lord is first
And all else is last.

# What Can Be Lost?

As I danced through the streets, my ankles bound in silver
The whole town thought I had gone mad.
She'll ruin the family, my mother-in-law cried,
And the prince sent me a cup of poison.
I laughed as I drank it—don't they understand?
How can you lose your body and mind
If the Dark One has already taken them?
He is the lifter of mountains,
And Mira is safe in him.

# Deserted

༺༻

Ah, the Dark One speaks not a word
Why should this body breathe? It's pointless.
Another night wasted, and he has not opened my dress.
Years pass and not one sign.
Everyone said, "He'll be here with the rains, don't worry."
I look out at thunder clouds shot with lightning,
And the ticking clock arouses such old dread.
Mira is a slave to her Lord
Her life one long night of craving.

# Rabindranath Tagore

## (1861–1941)

૭૭

The greatest modern Indian poet, Tagore won the Nobel Prize in 1913, only a year after the appearance of his book *Gitanjali* announced a voice of deep religious wisdom and lyric gifts. Tagore wrote in Bengali but had an enormous influence throughout the world. His talent extended to numerous plays, songs, novels, and paintings. Like the earlier *bhakti* poets to whom he owed a great debt (acknowledged when he translated his own versions of Kabir), Tagore is revered as a saint as well as an artist.

# Listen!

Listen, my heart, to the whispering of the world.
That is how it makes love to you.

# The Road

֍

I grew tired of the road
when it took me here and there.
I married it in love
when it took me Everywhere.

# Freshness

꧁꧂

How the desert yearns for the love of just one blade of grass!
The grass shakes her head, laughs, and flies away.

## My Sign

❦

My heart beats in waves
on the shore of the world
And writes its name in tears
with these words:
"I love you."

# Longing

What do I long for?
Something that is felt in the night
but not seen in the day.

# Radiance

&&

A cloud stood humbly in a corner of the sky.
The morning saw it and crowned it with splendor.

# A Touch

*☙❧*

I feel the night's beauty like a woman in love
When she puts out the light.

# Distant Words

꩜

"You send me love letters in the moon,"
The night said to the sun.
"And I leave you my answer
As tears upon the grass."

# A Request

☙

Indulge me a moment while I sit by your side.

Without a glimpse of your face, my heart cannot rest,
   and my work becomes drudgery in an endless sea of toil.
Today summer came to my window, sighing and
    murmuring, and the bees played like minstrels at the
    court of flowery groves.

Now we'll sit quietly, each to each,
   and sing our dedication to life
   in silent and ever-flowing ease.

## Until He Comes . . .

୭୧

I'm just waiting here for love
So he can have my surrender.

That's why it is so late
And I've left everything undone.
They came with their laws and rules
To tie me up and haul me away.
They cast their blame and cried,
"Can't you see what's wrong?"
Then the marketplace closed, and the day was done,
And everyone who came has had a fit and gone.

I'm just waiting here for love
So he can have my surrender.

# I Didn't Know

⚭

When the lotus opened, I didn't notice and went away
empty-handed.

Only now and again do I suddenly sit up from my dreams
to smell a strange fragrance. It comes on the south wind,
a vague hint that makes me ache with longing, like
the eager breath of summer wanting to be completed.
I didn't know what was so near, or that it was mine.

This perfect sweetness blossoming in the depths of my
heart.

# The Wayfarer

In the deep shadows of a rainy July
With secret steps you walk alone,
Silent as night, eluding all eyes.

The morning pays no attention to the call of the wind
A thick veil is thrown over the ever-watchful sky
The woods have hushed their songs
And at every house the door is shut
To the solitary wayfarer on this deserted street.

Oh, my only friend, my best beloved,
The gates are open at my house!
Don't pass me by like a dream.

# Longing

ගෙ

He came and sat by my bed
But I didn't wake up—
What a curse it is to sleep!
O miserable me!

He came when the night was still
With his harp in his hands
And the melodies he played
Sounded in my dreams.

Ah, why do I lose my nights?
Why do I miss the sight of him
Whose softest breath caresses my sleep?

# Forgetfulness

ೞ

Days go by when I forget to be ready
When you enter my heart unbidden like some stranger in
the crowd
And stamp the fleeting moments with eternity.

Today I came across one of them
And saw your mark, thrown with all the rest into the dust,
Where it mixed with the joys and sorrows of my trivial,
childish days
Totally forgotten.

Yet you didn't turn with contempt seeing me play in
the dust.
And the toddling steps I take in my nursery
Are the same steps that echo from star to star.

# This Is My Delight

## ✂

This is my delight, to watch and wait by the wayside,
As the shadow races the light
And the summer rain chases the sun.

Messengers greet me from unknown skies
Racing past on the road.
My heart is glad, the passing breeze is sweet,
Because I know that in one happy moment
I will see.

Meanwhile I sit before my door
Smiling and singing alone.
Meanwhile the air is filling with the sweet perfume
Of promise.

# O Let Me Sleep!

❦

The night is nearly gone, I've been waiting in vain.
What if he comes in the morning, when I'm wearily asleep?
Oh, leave the door open, don't turn him away,
But if his steps do not wake me, let me sleep, I pray.
Don't wake me with a choir of clattering birds
Or the noisy wind at the festival of morning.
Even if my lord is suddenly at the door
Let me sleep.

Ah sleep, precious sleep, that only waits for his touch!
My closed eyes that will open at the light of his smile
When he stands like a dream emerging from the dark.
Let him be like the first of all lights, the first of all forms,
The first thrill of joy to my awakened soul.
Let one glance from him do everything—
As I wake to myself, let me return on the instant
To him.

# The King and the Beggar

⊙

As I went begging today from door to door they cried, "He is coming! He draws near!" And seeing the dust of your gorgeous chariot, I thought, "Who can this be but a king among kings?"

My hopes soared, and I stood there waiting for alms to be given and wealth scattered in the dust. Your chariot stopped right before me, you looked down with a smile, and I knew that the luck of my days had come. Until suddenly you held out your palm and said, "What will you give?"

Begging from a beggar! What a kingly jest—I was confused and dismayed, but I groped in my sack until I brought out one grain of wheat, the tiniest thing I could afford.

I got home that night and emptied my sack on the floor,
only to spy a grain of gold gleaming there in the heap. Then
how bitterly I wept. *If you did this for a tiny grain of wheat,
what would you return if I had given you everything?*

## Instead of a Rose

೦೧

I wanted the roses you wore around your neck, but I
    was afraid.
After you left I scrambled for a flower in the bed,
Like a beggar at dawn I searched for a petal or two.

Ah me, what is this? What token has my lover left?
No flower, no spice, no vase of perfumed water,
But a sword, flashing like flame, heavy as a thunderbolt.
The young light of morning creeps in the window,
    spreading over the bed,
And twittering birds cry, "Woman, what have you there?"

I sit and muse with wonder—what is this gift of yours?
I have no place to hide it, I am ashamed to wear it, so frail
    am I,
It hurts me when I press it to my breast.
Yet in my heart I shall wear it with honor, this burden
    of pain,
This thy gift.

From this moment I will fear nothing in the world,

And you shall be victorious in all my strife.

Your sword is with me to cut my bonds asunder.

Away with being decorated like a doll!

This is adornment enough.

You have left Death for my companion, and I shall crown
him with my life.

# Deliverance

⊙⊙

I won't be delivered by renouncing the world
My freedom is found in a thousand bonds of delight.
You fill this vessel to the brim
With color and perfume, my world lights
Its hundred lamps with your flame
And lays them on the altar of your temple.

No, the doors of my senses will never be shut
What I see and hear and touch bears your delight
Until all my illusions turn into illuminations
And all my desires ripen into the fruits of love.

# Imperfect

৩৩

On the first day of creation, when the stars shone in new
splendor
The gods drew near and cried, "Ah, the picture of
perfection, not a blemish in this joy!"
But one of them suddenly said, "I feel a break in the chain
of light, one of the stars has been lost."
The strings of the golden harp snapped, their song died, and
they clamored in dismay,
"That one lost star was the best of all, the glory of heaven."
From that day forth the search never ends, and the cry goes
forth
That in one mislaid star the earth lost its joy.
Only in the deep stillness of the night do the stars smile
and whisper to each other,
"They're all looking in vain. Everywhere we look there is
only perfection."

# One Touch

∞

I look in every corner, desperate with hope,
    but she's not there.
My house is so small, anything I lose
    won't be coming back.
But your house is infinite, Lord, and seeking her
    has brought me to your door.
I stand under the golden canopy of the evening sky
    lifting my eyes to you
Here at the brink of eternity, nothing vanishes—
    not hope or happiness or the sight of her face
    seen through tears.
Now dip my empty life into your ocean
Plunge me into its deepest fullness!
And I shall feel her sweet lost touch
    in the cosmic All.

## The Flower and the Fruit

When I was young, my life was like a flower
That tosses a petal or two away
When the spring wind comes to beg at her door.

Now my life is like a fruit
With nothing to spare,
Waiting to offer myself completely
In the full burden of my sweetness.

## Letter from You

୭୯

I awoke and the morning brought me a letter
Which I can't read, since I don't know how.
I'll just hold it to my forehead, press it to my heart.
When the night grows still and the stars appear one by one
I'll spread it on my lap and be silent.
The rustling leaves will read it to me then,
The rushing steam will chant its words,
And the seven wise stars will sing from the sky.

I'll never find what I'm looking for,
Or understand what I should learn,
But this letter still unread has lightened my burden
And turned all my thoughts into song.

## Pathless Path

ॐ

I lost my way where the roads are laid,
No hint of a trail in the wide water or the sky,
The path was hidden by birds' wings, the fiery stars,
  and blooms of a wayfaring season.
So I asked of my heart,
"Do you carry some wisdom in the blood
Of an unseen Way?"

# The Unseen Hand

It's not for you to unfurl the buds.
Shake them, hit them—you have no power
To make them blossom.
You soil them with your touch,
Tearing the petals and scattering them in the dust.
No colors appear, no perfume—
Ah, it's not for you to do that!

He who can open a bud does it simply
One glance, and the sap must stir,
One breath, and a flower flutters in the wind,
Colors flash out like longings of the heart,
And perfume betrays sweet secrets.
He who can open a bud does it simply.

# Awaiting

ஓஓ

One day I will meet the life within me,
the joy hiding inside, my days perplexed
like a path in the dust.
I will know it by glimpses and fitful breaths
That make my thoughts fragrant for a while.

One day I will meet the joy outside me
dwelling behind this screen of light.
Then I shall stand in overflowing solitude
Where all is seen by the Creator.

## Poverty

ഌ൙

The sky smiled when you dressed me in rags
And sent my heart begging from door to door.
She walked the dust of the road
And when her bowl seemed all but full
Robbers took it all.

The weary day closed—
She came to your door with her pitiful bowl.
Out you came and took her hand
To seat her beside you on a throne.

# The Sculptor

ꙮ

When I thought to make your image
So people could worship it,
I molded it from my dust and desires,
Colored with delusion and dreaming.

Then I asked you to make an image of me
That you could love,
And you molded it from your own stuff:
Fire and might, truth, beauty, and peace.

# Defiled

ⓧ

It made me sick, O beautiful Lord, when they dirtied your
     robe in mirth.

I looked up and cried, "Lift thy rod of punishment and
     judge them."

So the morning light struck their eyes, red from a drunken
     night.

A white lily filled their stinking breath, and the stars in
     sacred darkness gazed upon their mad carousing.

That's how you treated those who dirtied your robe.


But in their reckless greed they climbed your gates
     robbing the riches of your storehouse.

Until the weight of their plunder grew too heavy to
     bear away.

I cried out, "Forgive them, O terrible one!"

Then you burst out in storms, scattering their theft in
     the dust.

In thunder was your forgiveness, in a shower of blood,
     and the angry red of sunset.

## Lost and Found

❧

Today I found some old letters of mine
stuffed in a box—
She'd saved them up as trinkets
for memory to play with.
As if her timid heart
standing against the tumult of time
said, "These are mine!"

No one's left to claim them now,
or pay the price of husbandry,
yet here they are.
Surely some love there is
that will save her from loss out there
just as she saved these letters
with such utmost care.

# Loving Prayer

Woman, bring beauty into my lonely life
Just as you once did in my house.
Sweep away the dust of hours,
Fill the empty lamps,
And mend all this, my neglect.
Then open the door of the shrine,
Light one candle, and in silence we'll be joined
Before our God.

# A Woman's Touch

☙❧

That moment when you touched me
I saw a mystery at the heart of creation.
A woman returns to God his flow of sweetness,
The freshness and beauty of days,
The dance in a bubbling stream,
The song in the morning light.
With heaving breast she suckles the thirsty earth,
And when the Eternal One breaks in two,
From a joy that cannot contain itself,
Woman is that overflow,
The pain of love.

# Unity

❧❦

What rhythm is this that rocks the world?
We laugh when it beats upon the crest of life,
We quail in terror when it returns to darkness.
But the play is the same, the coming and going
Of one endless music.

# The One and the Many

Yours is the light that breaks from the dark,
The good that springs from divided hearts,
The house that opens out on the world,
The love that calls from the battlefield.

Your gift is a gain in the midst of loss,
The life that flows through the caverns of death.
Yours is the heaven that lies in the dust,
And when you are there for me,
You are there for us all.

# Only a Child

❦

She's still a child, running around the palace,
She plays and would make a toy even of you.
She doesn't notice when her hair comes undone
And her careless skirts drag in the dust.
She falls asleep when you call her,
And your morning flower slips from her hands.
When the storm breaks under darkening clouds,
She whimpers in bed and clings in terror.
She is most afraid of failing to serve you,
But you smile and indulge all her games,
Because you know her, and something else you know:
That the child sitting in the dust is destined to be a bride
When her play is stilled and deepens into love.

# Transcendence

ଡ଼ଔ

My mind trembles with the shimmering leaves.
My heart sings with the touch of sunlight.
My life is glad to be floating with all things
Into the blue of space and the dark of time.

# The Soul's Pain

❧

I feel this pang inside—
Is it my soul trying to break out,
Or the world's soul trying to break in?

# Returning

The earth was kissed by raindrops
who whispered,
"We are your homesick children, Mother,
coming back to you from heaven."

# Epitaph

☙❧

When I die the world will be silent about me,
Keeping behind only one word: "I have loved."

*Dear Friend,*

I would like to invite you to visit
http://www.mypotential.com, where you may
join me on a journey of exploration and self-
discovery. Our mission at MyPotential is to
create programs and content to help people lead
healthier, more fulfilling, and more meaningful
lives. On a daily basis, we hope that through
MyPotential we can offer wisdom, inspiration,
and practical tools to help bring your highest
aspirations to fruition. I look forward to meeting
you at the MyPotential community.

*Much love,*

Deepak